Communion
of the
Sick

I
Can

F

McCrimmons
Great Wakering, Essex

First published in Great Britain in 1975 by
Mayhew-McCrimmon Ltd. Great Wakering, Essex

Revised edition © 1996 by
McCRIMMON PUBLISHING COMPANY LTD,
10-12 High Street, Great Wakering, Essex SS3 0EQ
Telephone 01702 218956

ISBN 0 85597 488 5

Concordatcum originali John P. Dewis

Acknowledgements

English translation of the Rite of Anointing and Pastoral Care of the Sick, ©1982, International Committee on English in the Liturgy,

Scripture readings are taken from the Jerusalem Bible version of the Scriptures, copyright ©1966, 1967 and 1968, Darton, Longman and Todd Ltd. and Messrs Doubleday and Sons. Used by permission.

Psalms: by permission of the Grail.

The version of the Psalms is that translated from the Hebrew by the Grail, copyright ©1963, The Grail (England) and published by William Collins and Sons Ltd in 'The Psalms: A New Translation'.
Used by permission.

Cover design by Mark Poulter
Typesetting by McCrimmon Publishing Company Ltd.
Printed by BPC Wheatons Ltd, Exeter

CONTENTS

INTRODUCTION

One of the clearest and dearest memories that the Christian community has of the Lord Jesus is of his love and care of the sick. One of the most important commissions that the Lord gave to his disciples and to the Church was to minister to the sick. Indeed in Matthew's gospel we are reminded that Christ's love for the sick is such that he makes himself one with them, so that to minister to the sick is to minister to Christ. "I was sick and you visited me." "When did we do this?" "… in so far as you did this to the least of these brothers and sisters of mine, you did it to me."

Jesus' ministry to the sick, that we are invited to make our own, was a ministry that included a care for physical healing but went deeper still. There was a concern for the healing of the person themselves, physically and spiritually, and also a healing of the breach between the person and their society. Then as now the sick were often pushed to the fringes of society; then isolated beyond city walls, now isolated so often in their own homes or hospitals.

The isolation within society cruelly mirrors the isolation that the sick sometimes feel from the Lord. In truth he is close, at one with us in our suffering, but in our sickness we can feel abandoned, even punished, by God. The ministry of Jesus, the ministry that the Church is asked to make its own, seeks to reveal the lie of the evil one in this. We are not alone, punished. It just is not so. Jesus, with the full authority of God made one of us, spoke of the eternal love and healing that is God for us. He restored to the sick, as to all who are estranged, a present unity with the God of love who is always faithful, always loving, always merciful. The Church is asked to do the same.

Of course, the principal challenge to the Church is to show the love of God to the sick in the ordinary business of life. The care shown by a neighbour, by a parish visiting group, is an indispensable ministry that underpins and authenticates the ministry of word and sacrament. It shows there is more to the Church than just talk. It reminds us too that when we come to the celebration of the rites that the particular ministers here are a part of a team of ministers, and that the team is part of a parish that cares and in whose name they serve.

For Catholics an important part of the ritual of our lives is taking part in the Sunday celebration of mass. It is there that the community comes together to recognise Christ in our midst, in the community itself and in the word and sacrament. For the sick and the housebound this particular ritual is something they cannot take part in, and consequently so much is lost to them: the gathering with friends, and strangers; the opportunity to hear the word of God proclaimed; the opportunity to be joined with the whole community at the

Lord's table and together to be fed there with his body and blood. The rites in this book are there to help the rest of the Church to respond to that lack, to minister to the needs that are not being met in the usual ways.

SOME PRACTICAL HINTS FOR MINISTERS TO THE SICK

The day and the time for visiting the sick with communion

Sunday is the day the Church keeps sacred to the Lord, the day we gather for mass. It speaks clearly to the sick that they are truly of this community when they are remembered in prayer at the Sunday assembly and then the word and sacrament are brought them directly mass is finished. It also speaks clearly to the rest of the parish of the importance that the sick have in the community. Where it is not possible then, of course, communion can be taken to the sick from any mass, or from the reserved sacrament in the tabernacle. With regard to the time - whatever is most convenient for the sick person is best, of course. However the other commitments of ministers do have to be taken into consideration.

Carrying communion to the sick

The eucharistic bread should be carried in a pyx or small closed container. Sufficient hosts should be taken for the communion of the sick and those who are caring for them and who, for that reason, themselves may not have been able to take part in the main parish celebration. On occasion communion may need to be carried under the form of wine. Again there is need for care that a vessel is used which is closed in a way that avoids all danger of spilling.

Preparation of the place for communion

It is desirable that there should be some table or other surface covered with a cloth upon which the blessed sacrament will be placed. The lighting of candles is a familiar sign that we are celebrating the prayer of the Church. Often those who are housebound can themselves prepare the table and candles, and the preparation of the table can be a helpful way of preparing for the prayer. In other circumstances those caring for the sick person will be able to prepare this. Failing all else the minister can easily carry a corporal and candle to use.

The Ministry of the Word

The Lord comes to us in word and sacrament. And very often it is a word from the scriptures that provides us with something to meditate on and draw strength from in our sickness. The readings in this book are helpful especially for those who are in need of special ministry for a relatively short while. For those who are away from the regular assembly for a long time it may well prove more helpful to use the Sunday readings, and also to spend some time reflecting on the word together with the sick person, perhaps using some of the material from the Sunday homily. Those who are more seriously ill may benefit most from a very short reading, maybe even one line or phrase being repeated two or three times, prayerfully, helping them to find nourishment in it. It is interesting to note that in the same way as the minister of communion carries communion to the sick, so in some parishes the ministers of the word accompany them to 'carry' and minister the word to the sick. This can help to make the whole rite more prayerful.

Ministering communion

Normally communion is given in the form of the eucharistic bread. Sometimes it is not possible for a sick person to consume a whole host, in which case a smaller piece should be given. Often the swallowing of the host is difficult. If so, ensure that there is a glass of water to hand to assist the person in swallowing.

Prayer

It is relatively easy to focus on the things in the book that have to be done: the readings, the written prayers, the communion that has to be given. However the context of all these is prayer. Prayer is helped by the ritual form - we can quickly learn the pattern and know what comes next. However the ritual pattern is not all there is to the prayer. The rite allows ample opportunity for sitting quietly after the reading, after communion, for offering intercessory prayer. When one is sick it is not easy to focus on prayer. The presence of the minister, the structure of the rite often helps still the inner turmoil and helps one to turn to the Lord. The good minister of communion recognises this and allows the time and space for it to happen.

"Be still, and know that I am God."

This booklet contains two rites for the communion of the sick.

The first is that to be used in normal circumstances, in the homes of the sick with, where possible, their family and friends gathered around them.

The second is for use in hospitals and institutions where there are many communicants to visit and there is little time for each visit. Obviously ministers not being able to spend time with the sick is far from ideal, and those finding themselves in this situation would doubtless seek assistance from others so that this ministry may be carried out as fruitfully and worthily as possible. It may prove possible to gather the sick into a common room, in which case the ordinary rite should be used. However failing this, when the use of the shorter rite is necessary, the minister is encouraged to begin by preparing for taking communion by praying one of the opening antiphons in the church, hospital chapel, or first room visited. Then the minister gives communion to the sick in the way indicated in the rite. Should the need or possibility present itself any elements from the rite for ordinary circumstances may be used, for example a reading from the Scriptures, when ministering to particular patients. The concluding prayer may be said in the church, the hospital chapel, or the last room visited. No blessing is given.

Allen Morris

Father Allen Morris

COMMUNION IN ORDINARY CIRCUMSTANCES

INTRODUCTORY RITES
Greeting
Sprinkling with Holy Water
Penitential Rite

LITURGY OF THE WORD
Reading
Response
General Intercessions

LITURGY OF HOLY COMMUNION
Lord's Prayer
Communion
Silent Prayer
Prayer after Communion

CONCLUDING RITE
Blessing

INTRODUCTORY RITES

Greeting

The minister greets the sick person and the others present. One of the following may be used:

A The peace of the Lord be with you always.
R. And also with you.

B Peace be with you (this house) and with all who live here.
R. And also with you.

C The grace of our Lord Jesus Christ and the love of God and the fellowship of the Holy Spirit be with you all.
R. And also with you.

D The grace and peace of God our Father and the Lord Jesus Christ be with you.
R. And also with you.

The minister then place the blessed sacrament on the table, and all join in adoration.

Sprinkling with Holy Water

If it seems desirable, the priest or deacon may sprinkle the sick person and those present with holy water. One of the following may be used:

A Let this water call to mind our baptism into Christ, who by his death and resurrection has redeemed us.

B Like a stream in parched land, may the grace of the Lord refresh our lives.

If the sacrament of penance is now celebrated the penitential rite is omitted.

Penitential Rite

The minister invites the sick person and all present to join in the penitential rite, using these or similar words:

A My brothers and sisters, to prepare ourselves for this celebration, let us call to mind our sins.

B My brothers and sisters, let us turn with confidence to the Lord and ask his forgiveness for all our sins.

After a brief period of silence, the penitential rite continues using one of the following:

A Lord Jesus, you healed the sick:
Lord, have mercy.

R. Lord, have mercy.

Lord Jesus, you forgave sinners:
Christ, have mercy.

R. Christ, have mercy.
Lord Jesus, you give us yourself to heal us and bring us strength:
Lord, have mercy.

R. Lord, have mercy.

B All say:

I confess to almighty God,
and to you, my brothers and sisters,
that I have sinned through my own fault

They strike their breast.

in my thoughts and in my words,
in what I have done,
and in what I have failed to do;
and I ask blessed Mary, ever virgin,
all the angels and saints,
and you, my brothers and sisters,
to pray for me to the Lord our God.

The minister concludes the penitential rite with the following:

May almighty God have mercy on us,
forgive us our sins,
and bring us to everlasting life.

R. Amen.

LITURGY OF THE WORD

Reading

The word of God is proclaimed by one of those present or by the minister. An appropriate reading or one of the following readings may be used:

A A reading from the holy gospel according to John 6:51

Jesus says: "I am the living bread which has come down from heaven.
Anyone who eats this bread will live for ever;
and the bread that I shall give
is my flesh, for the life of the world."

This is the Gospel of the Lord.

B A reading from the holy gospel according to John 6:54-58

Jesus says:
"Anyone who does eat my flesh and drink my blood has eternal life,
and I shall raise him up on the last day.
For my flesh is real food
and my blood is real drink.
He who eats my flesh and drinks my blood lives in me
and I live in him.

As I, who am sent by the living Father,
myself draw life from the Father,
so whoever eats me will draw life from me.

This is the bread come down from heaven;
not like the bread our ancestors ate:
they are dead,
but anyone who eats this bread will live for ever."

This is the Gospel of the Lord.

C A reading from the holy gospel
according to John 14:6

Jesus says:
"I am the Way, the Truth and the Life.
No one can come to the Father except
through me."

This the Gospel of the Lord.

D A reading from the holy gospel
according to John 15:5

Jesus says:
"I am the vine,
you are the branches.
Whoever remains in me, with me in him,
bears fruit in plenty;
for cut off from me you can do nothing."

This is the Gospel of the Lord.

E A reading from the first letter of John 4:16

We ourselves have known and put our faith in
God's love towards ourselves.
God is love
and anyone who lives in love lives in God,
and God lives in him.

This is Word of the Lord.

Response

A brief period of silence may be observed after the reading of the word of God.
The minister may then give a brief explanation of the reading, applying it to the needs of the sick person and those who are looking after him or her.

General Intercessions

The general intercessions may be said. With a brief introduction the minister invites all those present to pray. After the intentions the minister says the concluding prayer. It is desirable that the intentions be announced by someone other than the minister.

LITURGY OF HOLY COMMUNION

Lord's Prayer

The minister introduces the Lord's Prayer in these or similar words:

A Now let us pray as Christ the Lord taught us:

B And now let us pray with confidence as Christ our Lord commanded:

All say: Our Father...

Communion

The minister shows the eucharistic bread to those present, saying:

A This is the bread of life.
Taste and see that the Lord is good.

B This is the Lamb of God
who takes away the sins of the world.
Happy are those who are called to his supper.

The sick person and all who are to receive communion say:

Lord, I am not worthy to receive you,
but only say the word and I shall be healed.

The minister goes to the sick person and, showing the blessed sacrament, says:

The body of Christ.

The sick person answers: "Amen," and receives communion.
Then the minister says:

The blood of Christ.

The sick person answers "Amen," and receives communion.

Others present who wish to receive communion then do so in the usual way.

After the conclusion of the rite, the minister cleanses the vessel as usual.

Silent Prayer

Then a period of silence may be observed.

Prayer after Communion

The minister says a concluding prayer. One of the following may be used:

Let us pray.

Pause for silent prayer, if this has not preceded.

A God our Father,
you have called us to share the one bread
and one cup
and so become one in Christ.

Help us to live in him that we may bear fruit,
rejoicing that he has redeemed the world.

We ask this through Christ our Lord.

R. Amen.

B All-powerful God,
we thank you for the nourishment you give us
through your holy gift.

Pour out your Spirit upon us
and in the strength of this food from heaven
keep us single-minded in your service.

We ask this in the name of Jesus the Lord.

R. Amen.

C All-powerful and ever-living God,
may the body and blood of Christ your Son
be for our brother/sister N.
a lasting remedy for body and soul.

We ask this through Christ our Lord.

R. Amen.

CONCLUDING RITE

Blessing

The priest or deacon blesses the sick person and the others present, using one of the following blessings. If, however, any of the blessed sacrament remains, he may bless the sick person by making a sign of the cross with the blessed sacrament, in silence.

A May God the Father bless you.
R. Amen.

May God the Son heal you.
R. Amen.

May God the Holy Spirit enlighten you.
R. Amen.

May almighty God bless you,
the Father, and the Son, + and the Holy Spirit.
R. Amen.

B May the Lord be with you to protect you.
R. Amen.

May he guide you and give you strength.
R. Amen.

May he watch over you, keep you in his care,
and bless you with his peace.
R. Amen.

May almighty God bless you,
the Father, and the Son, + and the Holy Spirit.
R. Amen.

C May the blessing of almighty God,
the Father, and the Son, + and the Holy Spirit,
come upon you and remain with you for ever.
R. Amen.

A minister who is not a priest or deacon invokes God's blessing and makes the sign of the cross on himself or herself, while saying:

A May the Lord bless us,
protect us from all evil,
and bring us to everlasting life.
R. Amen.

B May the almighty and merciful God bless and protect us,
the Father, and the Son, and the Holy Spirit.
R. Amen.

COMMUNION IN A HOSPITAL OR INSTITUTION

A SIMPLIFIED RITE OF COMMUNION

It is sometimes the case that people are just too ill to benefit from a liturgy of the word and to be able to join in intercessory prayer.
On occasion one might have to take communion to a good number of people in hospital wards and simply not have time for the fuller ministry of the word. Were this latter case to be a frequent occurrence it would of course be preferable to try to build up the number of ministers able to assist in the ministry of the word and sacrament to the sick.
However where such situations arise and it is not practical to celebrate the fuller rite this simplified rite will be helpful.

PREPARATION

A preparation of oneself by reading one of the scripture passages on pp.14-16 and/or pp.24-32.

LITURGY OF HOLY COMMUNION

Greeting to each person visited
(using one of the greetings found on p.11)

Lord's Prayer

Communion of the sick person
(using the form found on p.17)

CONCLUDING PRAYER

This prayer may be said either in the last room visited, in the church or chapel.

A God our Father,
you have called us to share the one bread and one cup and so become one in Christ.
Help us to live in him
that we may bear fruit,
rejoicing that he has redeemed the world.
We ask this through Christ our Lord.
R. Amen.

B All powerful and ever-living God,
may the body and blood of Christ your Son
be for our brothers and sisters
a lasting remedy for body and soul.
We ask this through Christ our Lord.
R. Amen.

ADDITIONAL READINGS AND PSALMS

1. ELIJAH FORTIFIED BY THE BREAD OF GOD

Only God can give us the true nourishment we need for the strength to come to him.

A reading from the first book of Kings 19:4-8

The prophet Elijah, fleeing from the wrath of Jezebel, went into the wilderness, a day's journey, and sitting under a furze bush wished he were dead. "Lord," he said, "I have had enough. Take my life; I am no better than my ancestors." Then he lay down and went to sleep. But an angel touched him and said, "Get up and eat." He looked round, and there at his head was a scone baked on hot stones, and a jar of water. He ate and drank and then lay down again. But the angel of the Lord came back a second time and touched him and said, "Get up and eat, or the journey will be too long for you." So he got up and ate and drank, and strengthened by that food he walked for forty days and forty nights until he reached Horeb, the mountain of God.

2. WHO CAN SEPARATE US FROM THE LOVE OF CHRIST?

Whatever trials or suffering we may have to undergo, we shall overcome them in Christ, because of his love.

A reading from the letter of Saint Paul to the Romans 8:31-35/ 37-39

With God on our side who can be against us? Since God did not spare his own Son, but gave him up to benefit us all, we may be certain, after such a gift, that he will not refuse anything he can give. Could anyone accuse those that God has chosen? When God acquits, could anyone condemn? Could Christ Jesus? No! He not only died for us - he rose from the dead, and there at God's right hand he stands and pleads for us.

Nothing can come between us and the love of Christ, even if we are troubled or worried, or being persecuted, or lacking food or clothes, or being threatened or even attacked. These are the trials through which we triumph, by the power of him who loved us.

For I am certain of this: neither death nor life, no angel, no prince, nothing that exists, nothing still to come, not any power, or height or depth, nor any created thing, can ever come between us and the love of God made visible in Christ Jesus our Lord.

3. GOD MAKES US LIVE AGAIN BY GRACE

God loves us. He once gave new life to his exiled people, and now he makes us live again by the gift of Christ. Our existence should be a response to this free gift of God.

A reading from the first letter of Saint Paul to the Ephesians 2:4-5.6-10

God loves us with so much love that he was generous with his mercy: when we were dead through our sins, he brought us to life with Christ - it is through grace that you have been saved - and raised us up with him and gave us a place with him in heaven, in Christ Jesus.
This was to show for all ages to come, through his goodness towards us in Christ Jesus, how infinitely rich he is in grace. Because it is by grace that you have been saved, through faith; not by anything of your own, but by a gift from God; not by anything that you have done, so that nobody can claim the credit. We are God's work of art, created in Christ Jesus to live the good life as from the beginning he had meant us to live it.

4. TO LOVE IN TRUTH

To live faithfully under God's guidance, to love our sisters and brothers by doing what is right: such are the commands of the Lord of which Saint

John reminds us. We lay the foundation for the integrity of our lives by responding to them.

A reading from the first letter of Saint John 3:18-24

My children,
our love is not to be just words or mere talk,
but something real and active;
only by this can we be certain
that we are the children of the truth
and be able to quieten our conscience in his presence,
whatever accusations it may raise against us,
because God is greater than our conscience and he knows everything.
My dear people,
if we cannot be condemned by our own conscience,
we need not be afraid in God's presence,
and whatever we ask him,
we shall receive,
because we keep his commandments
and live the kind of life that he wants.
His commandments are these:
that we believe in the name of his Son Jesus Christ
and that we love one another
as he told us to.
Whoever keeps his commandments
lives in God and God lives in him.
We know that he lives in us
by the Spirit that he has given us.

5. GOD IS LOVE

God first showed love for us, by sending his Son. By loving our sisters and brothers, we associate ourselves in that love, and have true life.

A reading from the first letter of Saint John 4:7-10

My dear people,
let us love one another
since love comes from God
and everyone who loves is begotten by God
and knows God.
Anyone who fails to love can never have known God,
because God is love.
God's love for us was revealed
when God sent into the world his only Son
so that we could have life through him;
this is the love I mean:
not our love for God,
but God's love for us when he sent his Son
to be the sacrifice that takes our sins away.

6. THE PARADOX OF HAPPINESS IN THE GOSPEL

We are all searching for the way to happiness. Christ replies by giving us the beatitudes, which call on us to make a continual 'change of heart', so that we come to resemble him more and more.

A reading from the holy Gospel according to Saint Matthew 5:1-12

Seeing the crowds, Jesus went up the hill. There he sat down and was joined by his disciples. Then he began to speak. This is what he taught them:
"How happy are the poor in spirit:
theirs is the kingdom of heaven.
Happy the gentle:
they shall have the earth for their heritage.
Happy those who mourn:
they shall be comforted.
Happy those who hunger and thirst for what is right:
they shall be satisfied.
Happy the merciful:
they shall have mercy shown them.
Happy the pure in heart:
they shall see God.
Happy the peacemakers:
they shall be called sons of God.
Happy those who are persecuted in the cause of right:
theirs is the kingdom of heaven.
"Happy are you when people abuse you and persecute you and speak all kinds of calumny against you on my account. Rejoice and be glad, for your reward will be great in heaven."

7. THE CALMING OF THE STORM

People are always afraid and lack faith; but Christ, whose power calmed the tempest, knows where he is leading us. We can have confidence in him, even if he gives no sign of his presence.

A reading from the holy Gospel according to Saint Mark 4:35-41

With the coming of evening, Jesus said to his disciples "Let us cross over to the other side." And leaving the crowd behind him, they took him, just as he was, in the boat; and there were other boats with him. Then it began to blow a gale and the waves were breaking into the boat so that it was almost swamped. But he was in the stern, his head on the cushion, asleep. They woke him and said to him: "Master, do you not care? We are going down!" And he woke up and rebuked the wind and said to the sea: "Quiet now! Be calm!" And the wind dropped, and all was calm again. Then he said to them: "Why are you so frightened? How is it that you have no faith?" They were filled with awe and said to one another: "Who can this be? Even the wind and sea obey him."

8. HOPE IN THE LORD Psalm 27

The Lord is my light and my help;
whom shall I fear?
The Lord is the stronghold of my life;
before whom shall I shrink?
There is one thing I ask of the Lord, for this I long,
to live in the house of the Lord,

all the days of my life,
to savour the sweetness of the Lord,
to behold his temple.
For there he keeps me safe in his tent
in the day of evil.
He hides me in the shelter of his tent,
on a rock he sets me safe.
I am sure I shall see the Lord's goodness
in the land of the living.
Hope in him, hold firm and take heart.
Hope in the Lord!

9. THE GOODNESS OF THE LORD Psalm 33:1-9

I will bless the Lord at all times,
his praise always on my lips;
in the Lord my soul shall make its boast.
The humble shall hear and be glad.
Glorify the Lord with me.
Together let us praise his name.
I sought the Lord and he answered me;
from all my terrors he set me free.
Look toward him and be radiant;
let your faces not be abashed.
This poor man called; the Lord heard him
and rescued him from all his distress.
The angel of the Lord is encamped
around those who revere him, to rescue them.
Taste and see that the Lord is good.
He is happy who seeks refuge in him.

10. THE GREATNESS AND GOODNESS OF GOD

Psalm 144:8-9. 13b-16. 17-21

The Lord is kind and full of compassion,
slow to anger, abounding in love.
How good is the Lord to all,
compassionate to all his creatures.
The Lord is faithful in all his words
and loving in all his deeds.
The Lord supports all who fall
and raises all who are bowed down.
The eyes of all creatures look to you
and you give them their food in due time.
You open wide your hand,
grant the desires of all who live.
The Lord is just in all his ways
and loving in all his deeds.
He is close to all who call him,
who call on him from their hearts.
He grants the desires of those who fear him,
he hears their cry and he saves them.
The Lord protects all who love him;
but the wicked he will utterly destroy.
Let me speak the praise of the Lord,
let all mankind bless his holy name
for ever, for ages unending.